A MIND Transformed

A **30-DAY DEVOTIONAL** TO **CONQUER THE STRUGGLE**
AND **RECLAIM THE POWER** OVER YOUR THOUGHTS

CRYSTAL CAMPBELL

Copyright © 2020 by Crystal Campbell

A Mind Transformed: A 30-Day Devotional to Conquer the Struggle and Reclaim the Power over your Thoughts

ISBN: 978-1-7362463-0-6

Free Gift

Thank you so much for purchasing this book! As my gift to you, I'd like to give you the accompanying workbook. Please visit https://mailchi.mp/5b8eec2ade32/a-mind-transformed-workbook to receive it!

Dedication

This book is dedicated to my father, Vernon Dunn who always spoke this blessing over me, "The pure in heart shall see God." To my first church, Berean Baptist Church that taught me Greater is He that was in me than he that is in the world. To my husband, John Campbell III, for pushing me into purpose. And to my children, Johanna & John, who inspire me to be better daily.

Contents

Preface

Are you torn between what your flesh craves and what your spirit needs? Do you feel victim to your own desires? Do you want to overcome strongholds and find lasting victory? Then this book is for you! On the following pages you will find hope to rediscover who you are, why you were created, and what you are here to do. Learn the truth that in the kingdom, nothing is ever really wasted just repurposed for God's glory and for your gain. Gain tools to unlock the potential within and become a new creation by changing the way you think. I pray that God will exceed your expectations and bring transformation as you renew your mind in Him.

A little into why I choose to write this book. I was only a young girl when I was first introduced to an adult magazine. I could feel that seeing what I was looking at us was wrong. Later in life when I was in my early teens, I had the opportunity to watch pornography when I was away from home. This created a desire in me to see more. Church was big deal growing up, which gave me a spiritual foundation and allowed God to war for my soul. His word became a passion in me that conflicted with the passions of my flesh. I was raised to believe that God was real but I had yet to accept him as my Lord. One day after hearing a minister speak, the Holy Spirit hit me like a wave and I knew that I needed God in life and I needed to surrender my life to Him. After asking Jesus into my heart, I asked him to deliver me from lust and He did! But it was not an overnight process – God can choose to heal in time or over time. He took me on a journey in his word of knowing why I was created, what my body was meant for, and how I should treat others. He set down roots in his word and gave me a foundation to build on. He renewed my mind.

It doesn't take long to look around and see the impact that our tainted hearts have had on our world. Human Trafficking - the practice of exploiting adults and children for use as commodities, or objects, in conditions of sexual and labor servitude has become a 150-billion dollar industry. Pornography has gripped minds and hearts through visual prostitution. It has an estimated profit of 10-15 billion in the US, and 97 billion worldwide. Although these stats may just seem like numbers on a page, most of us have had a personal experience or been privy to the heartbreak they bring. Countless lives have been impacted, marriages and families torn apart by not allowing God's word to change us from the inside out.

It's time to confront the ugly truth that our private behavior has public consequences. The struggle is real but nothing that our God cannot handle. We can overcome and have victory in our thoughts and lives! The bible says in 1Corinthians 10:13 "No temptation has overtaken you except such as is common to man; but God is faithful, who will not allow you to be tempted beyond what you are able, but with the temptation will also make the way of escape, that you may be able to bear it." We have the choice of both good and evil so we must be intentional on choosing good. In doing so, we can experience healing, walk in authority, and set a new precedence for our families, businesses, and world culture.

Author's Declaration

As you read these pages, I pray you are encouraged that you are not alone. We have all played the fool; living as though there is no GOD. Some for a little while and others for an extended period of time. Regardless of your status, God wants to transform the way you think. Whether your innocence was taken from you or you gave it away freely, there is restoration found in Jesus, our great redeemer. This journey, though a deeply personal one has wonderful rippling effects. For the destination to a new you, begins with a journey to a new mind.

This devotional is broken into 3 sections: God's Preeminence, My Predestination, and Others' Perfection allowing you to understand the connection between your relationships with God, yourself, and others. At the end of each devotion is a prayer, reflection questions, and scriptures to meditate on. The word of God says, "I have hidden your word in my heart, that I may not sin against you." Psalms 119:11 Feel free to meditate on the scriptures in this book to lead you to a deeper, more initimate walk with your heavenly father and experience the transformation that your heart desires.

Theme Scripture

Do not be conformed to this world but continuously be transformed by the renewing of your mind so that you may be able to determine what God's will is- what is proper, pleasing, and perfect!
– Romans 12:2(ISV)

God's Preeminence

God's Providence

Oh Lord, thou hast searched me and known me.
                                        –Psalms 139:1 (KJV)

When I think about how God is all knowing and all seeing, I am in awe. The truth that there is a being that not only sees external action but also internal motives…! Normally this is not the type of insight that I share with people. As it relates to my dirty laundry, I prefer to pile it up until it can barely stand and drape a clean white cloth over it for everyone to see. But God has a way of getting past all that. The scripture unfolds in verses 2-3 when it says, "He knows our down sitting and our uprising and is intimately acquainted with all my ways." I can hide nothing from Him, which is a little scary but on the other hand very refreshing. In a world where we are constantly trying to get others to understand us, see our point of view. God gets it! He gets us. He knows everything about us and He still loves us. Now that's amazing!! He is our closest confidant, our most loyal friend, and a faithful father. One that when He created us made us on purpose and for a purpose. Jer. 29:11 says "I know the plans I have for you. Plans to prosper you, to give you a hope and a future." God is always going to call the good out of you because he knows it's in you, He put it there! So, the next time you are uncomfortable with the all-knowing, providential nature of God. Just know that He has a good plan for you and the reason He keeps confronting you with your mess is that He wants you to know the you, He already knows.

Pray

Father God, search my heart. Show me any place in me that I have tried to keep separate from you. I understand that the only way for me to clean up my mess is to uncover it. I thank you that you are not overly critical of me and only correct me because you love me. Help me to always remember that you have great plans for me and that you will assist me to walk them out. You are a great God, help me to yield my way to your better way.

In Jesus name, Amen

Reflect

❖ What are some things in my life that I have tried to hide from God?

❖ How does knowing there is a purpose for my life change how I view God's instruction?

Meditate

And we know that in all things God works for the good of those who love him, who have been called according to his purpose. –Romans 8:28

In their heart's humans plan their course, but the LORD establishes their steps. –Proverbs 16:9

The lot is cast into the lap, but its every decision is from the LORD. –Proverbs 16:33

Day 2

God's Provision

But my God shall supply all your need according to his riches in glory by Christ Jesus.
                                                             –Phil 4:19(KJV)

We live in a supply and demand culture. Whatever the world demands must be supplied and by any means necessary, sometimes at any cost. Because of this world view, the lines have been blurred between need and want. This causes us to label something a need when actually it's only a want. However, God knows what we are truly in need of and is ready to fulfill those needs in such an amazing way. Because we serve an all-knowing God, he is able to supply our needs in a holistic way. He supplies clothes for our covering and peace for our souls. Food for our nourishment and joy for our hearts, shelter for our protection and wisdom for our minds. With such a generous God, it is strange we don't ask for what he has already provided. The word provision means to prepare beforehand, meaning God already prepared what you and I would stand in need of and made preparation to help. Temptation to sin is no different. 1 Cor. 10:13 "No temptation has overtaken you except what is common to mankind." Even though temptation may come often, God will consistently offer a way out. However, it is up to you and I to take it. Because we are made in the image of God, we too have the power to create provision. You can set yourself up for success by making provision to live a Godly life. Putting things in place so you are less likely to fall. Rom. 13:14 says "Instead, clothe yourself with the Lord Jesus Christ and do not think about how to gratify the desires of the flesh." Know that God will and has provided everything you need according to His riches and glory. If given the option, to let God provide or try to provide for myself. I choose God!

Pray

Lord, your provision is boundless and there is no end to your supply. You are always thinking ahead and have already made plans for me. I thank you that I don't have to worry or be anxious about getting my needs met or strive to make them happen by myself. Help me to not place myself in compromising situations that weaken my ability to stand strong in you. When I am tempted to go my own way help me to look for the way out that you have already prepared for me. I release control of my life and what I believe I need and I trust you to provide in ways that I could have never imagine.

In Jesus name, Amen

Reflect

❖ How does knowing God will provide what I need free me from worry?

❖ In what areas do I need to release control of meeting my own needs?

Meditate

And God is able to bless you abundantly, so that in all things at all times, having all that you need, you will abound in every good work. −2 Corinthians 9:8

But seek first his kingdom and his righteousness, and all these things will be given to you as well. −Matthew 6:33

If you, then, though you are evil, know how to give good gifts to your children, how much more will your Father in heaven give good gifts to those who ask him! −Matthew 7:11

Day 3

God's Protection

Whoever dwells in the shelter of the Most High will rest in the shadow of the Almighty.

-Psalm 91:1 *(NIV)*

When I think of a secret place, I think of something hidden from the natural eye. An exclusive destination. Have you ever seen a movie where the character goes through a sliding door or underground tunnel that no-one knew was there? I believe that is what God's protection is like. Outsiders see the chaos around us but we are tucked away in the joy of the Lord. People can't quite figure out how we remain so calm. The bible says in 2 Cor. 10:3 "For though we live in the world, we do not wage war as the world does." In this life there are many things that can cause us to fear but we must realize that there is an unseen battle going on. We have forces working against us: trying to steal, kill, and destroy our God-given purpose. We need the power of God to keep us safe from the tricks and traps of the enemy. Sin lures us in like a spider's web, offering fun and adventure. However, we then find ourselves stuck in its maze, unable to break free. Thanks be to God who is able to untangle us from our sticky mess and set us free! God has left us His word to give us instruction and wisdom that we may walk in His paths and protective care. God has also set eternity in our hearts, (Eccl. 3:11) so that we may know there is so much more to life than its temporary pleasures. There is overwhelming protection for those who walk in His Will. God says, "Though a thousand shall fall at your side and ten thousand at your right hand, no danger shall come near you." Psalm. 91:7 So pray and ask God for a mind to seek, a heart to do, and a soul that yields to His Will.

Pray

Father God, thank you for divine protection. Give me a heart to believe that you know what is best for me. Open my eyes to see your hand at work in protecting me from harm and danger. Since I know that there is an enemy trying to deter me from your plan for my life, help me to hide in the protective custody of your instruction. Make me awake to the truth that there is more to this life than the here and now. I know that when I choose to remain in your care, your council will guide me and keep me safe.

In Jesus Name, Amen

Reflect

❖ How can trusting in God's word keep me from danger?

❖ What are some ways I can see God protecting me?

Meditate

Put on the full armor of God, so that you can take your stand against the devil's schemes. –Ephesians 6:11

God is our refuge and strength, an ever-present help in trouble. –Psalms 46:1

Be strong and courageous. Do not be afraid or terrified because of them, for the LORD your God goes with you; he will never leave you nor forsake you." –Deut. 31:6

God's Wisdom

For who knows a person's thoughts except their own spirit within them? In the same way no one knows the thoughts of God except the Spirit of God.

–1 Cor. 2:11 (NIV)

Concentrate all your thoughts upon the work at hand. The sun's rays do not burn until brought to a focus. Alexander Graham Bell

Wisdom is a funny thing. Some people will see an opportunity and jump on it, yet others will perceive it as dangerous and run from it, and few will not comprehend or realize what is going on at all. I myself have been on both ends of the spectrum. I've been as sharp as a tack and as dull as a doorknob. If you're honest with yourself, you've had those experiences too. It is from these life experiences that we derive wisdom. Past experiences teach us how to be better equipped the next time we face an issue. The bible says "The fear of the Lord, is the beginning of wisdom." Prov. 9:10 It's not a spooky fear but a reverence fear that says God is God, and I am not. Let me listen and do what He says because He knows better than I do. The book of Proverbs is filled with directives that teach and if we let it, also train us to walk in wisdom.

Staying away from sexual immorality and keeping ourselves pure - body, mind, and soul is God's wisdom at work. Actively keeping us from the things that destroy us, our dreams, and even our families. God is interested in us leaving a legacy for future generations. A legacy of godliness and holiness, one that says I can be in this world, and not be of it. You can successfully avoid the pit falls that come to take you out of the race and **You can win**. It takes our cooperation to walk like the wise people we are. God says if we lack wisdom to ask for more and that He would give to us liberally. So, let us ask Him and seek the truth in His word so that we can walk in the good life freely given to us.

Pray

Lord, you are so much bigger and wiser than I ever thought. Your ways escape words. I reverence you for who you are and I lay down my agenda for your wise plans. Holy Spirit please give me understanding of your ways so that I can see things from your perspective. Give me wisdom to make better decisions and help me to make them with your purpose for me in mind.

In Jesus Name, Amen

Reflect

❖ What have been some results of following my own wisdom instead of God's?

❖ How can I make better decisions by following God's way of doing things?

Meditate

Be very careful, then, how you live--not as unwise but as wise, making the most of every opportunity, because the days are evil. –Ephesians 5:15-16

But the wisdom that comes from heaven is first of all pure; then peace-loving, considerate, submissive, full of mercy and good fruit, impartial and sincere. –James 3:17

The one who gets wisdom loves life; the one who cherishes understanding will soon prosper. –Proverbs 19:8

Day 5

God's Wonder

When I consider your heavens, then work of your fingers, the moon and the stars, which you have set in place, what is mankind that you are mindful of him, human beings that you care for them?
-Psalms 8:3-4 (NIV)

Wonder is a place of dreams and imagination. Where our curiosity and creative side connect. When something is full of wonder we call it wonderful. Even the happiest place on earth, Disney World is called a wonderland. However, there is a place where wonder derives and has its roots, and that is in God. The author of the scripture says when he looks at everything that God created, he cannot understand why God would be so concerned with man. Ever wonder why you are here? What's the point of your existence? Well, I'm here to tell you that you are the epitome of God's creation. "So, God created mankind in his own image, in the image of God he created them; male and female he created them." Gen. 1:27 Since we were made in God's image, for his unique purpose we need him to instruct us on how to carry it out. In order to do that, we need to have a reverence for God and a willingness to submit to His authority. Submission is not when you live under someone's rule and it is not a separate submission under the actual mission. It is simply when we yield our will to the will of the Father. God's plan for you is absolutely wonderful! You will not find another, including your own that can compare to the fulfillment you'll receive by completing God's plan for your life. So, let Him teach and direct you how you should walk. Then yield to the God that created everything on earth, but the only thing He saw worth dying for was you! Once you do, you will be in awe and filled with wonder of the good plan God has laid out just for you.

Pray

Father God, the more I know about you, the more you amaze me. The scope of who you are is incomparable. Yet you seem to have positioned me in your heart as a top priority. Give me the desire to know you in a more intimate way. Show me what it means to reverence you and submit to your authority. Of all the things that I may wonder about, may I never wonder about your love for me.

In Jesus name, Amen

Reflect

❖ How can I reprioritize my day to put God first?

❖ What are some new things I have learned about God by spending time with Him?

Meditate

This was the LORD's doing; It is marvelous in our eyes. –Psalms 118:23

Joshua told the people, "Consecrate yourselves, for tomorrow the LORD will do amazing things among you. –Joshua 3:5

For you are great and do marvelous deeds; you alone are God. –Psalms 86:10

Day 6

God Waits

The Lord is not slow in keeping His promise, as some understand slowness. Instead He is patient with you, not wanting anyone to perish, but everyone to come to repentance.
–2 Peter 3:9 (NIV)

There is no short of demand for patience these days, the ability to wait with joy and hope. Some would say it's a gift, others would call it a tool. But either way patience is something greatly desired. The key to having patience is expectation. Psalms 27:13 "I remain confident of this: I will see the goodness of the Lord in the land of the living." God expects great things of you and is therefore willing to wait until they manifest. He waits until we have had enough of sin and the results they produce. He waits until we are ready for real change and surrender our decisions over to Him. He waits until our maturity catches up to our destiny. He waits... When you see your Lord waiting patiently for you let it fill you with love and acceptance but let it also move you to expediency in doing the will of God. "Let us strip off every weight that slows us down, especially the sin that so easily trips us up." Heb. 12:1b Do not let any weight keep you from God's timing. It's your time to stop resisting and start repenting so you can move from the people whom He is waiting on to the people who await His return.

Pray

Father God, thank you for your patience with me. You have shown me that you will wait for me as long as it takes. Help me to wait on the things you said I could have and give me the right attitude of expectation as I wait. I want to get my hopes up on you. Help me to trust that I will see your goodness in my lifetime. May I either receive the desires of my heart or mature to the point that I no longer want anything outside of your will for me.

In Jesus name, Amen

Reflect

❖ Where can I look back in my life and see God's patience toward me?

❖ How does knowing that God is faithful to his promises help me to have patience?

Meditate

I wait for the LORD, my whole being waits, and in his word, I put my hope. —Psalms 130:5

Be still before the LORD and wait patiently for him; do not fret when people succeed in their ways, when they carry out their wicked schemes. —Psalms 37: 7

The LORD is good to those whose hope is in him, to the one who seeks him; —Lamentations 3:25

Day 7

God's Distinction

They have mouths, but cannot speak, eyes, but cannot see. They have ears, but cannot hear, nor is there breath in their mouths.
–Psalms 135:16-17 (NIV)

People are always trying to compare. We compare jobs, cars, houses, even spouses. We are on a constant search for the biggest, the brightest, and the baddest. We don't want anyone to know but secretly we want to be worshipped. Idols have a funny way of taking shape. They form whenever we put anything but God in first place in our lives. The bible says "He will not share His glory with anyone". Isaiah 42:8 God set himself apart by showing us who the true God is. In 1 Kings 18, there is an amazing display of God's power and authority. He sends fire from heaven, rain that people had not seen in years, and gave Elijah supernatural strength to outrun a chariot. He certainly showed up and showed out!

God wants us to know that He stands alone as the only true God is in our lives. Another way God distinguishes himself is in His humility. When Jesus' disciples asked, "who would be the greatest in the kingdom of heaven," He said "whoever is the servant on earth is the greatest in heaven." Matt. 18:1-4 He modeled this for us when he came down from heaven to die for us. We may have characterized distinction by outward accolades or appearance, but God is more interested with the heart. Our distinction comes from being created in God's image. It's the reason why God fights for you and the enemy fights against you and. You have been set apart for God's uniquely designed plan for your life. It's time to stand up and stand out for the one who stood up for you. Embrace your distinct identity as a child of the Most High God.

Pray

Lord, help me to identify with you more than anything or anyone else. I declare you are the one true God and anything that attempts to stand in your place is an imposter. Please forgive me for allowing my heart to stray. I am uniquely created in you, an original. Help me to embrace my identity as a child of God so that I can walk in the authority and peace-giving freedom that it brings.

In Jesus name, Amen

Reflect

❖ What changes do I need to make to have God be 1st place in my life?

❖ How does knowing I am child of God change how I see myself?

Meditate

There is no one holy like the LORD; there is no one besides you; there is no Rock like our God. −1 Sam. 2:2

God is not human, that he should lie, not a human being, that he should change his mind. Does he speak and then not act? Does he promise and not fulfill? −Num. 23:19

I am the LORD, and there is no other; apart from me there is no God. I will strengthen you, though you have not acknowledged me, −Isaiah 45:5

Day 8

God's Discipline

No discipline seems pleasant at the time, but painful. Later on, however, it produces a harvest of righteousness and peace for those who have been trained by it.
–Hebrews 12:11 (NIV)

My memories of being disciplined as a child is something I can look back and smile at now because of the foolish things I did. However, at the time they were stressful events. Though there are varying thoughts on discipline vs consequences, most will agree that when you do something wrong you need a course correction to get you back on track. Adam and Eve were our first examples of that course correction. God instructed them not to eat from the tree of good and evil for in the day they did, they would surely die. Gen. 2:16-17 The tempter came and told Eve, you will not surely die, but the day you do you will be like God. Genesis 3. As the story goes, she did eat and gave some to her husband. The fallout of their sin lead to hard work and hard labor and I would imagine, a firm reminder that listening to God's instruction is the best way to live. The temptation to be God, to be our own ruler is a false since if power. Adam and Eve did not need a piece of fruit, sweet and juicy as it may be, to be like God. They were already made in God's image and likeness. They didn't need to disobey God in order to know what was good. In the Garden of Eden, there was beauty and pleasure galore. What they didn't know was evil, the very thing he wanted to prevent them and us from experiencing. God is a good God. He doesn't instruct us to limit us but to make sure that our lives remain limitless. Sin has a hefty price tag; it promises pleasure but its results are painful. Many lives have been destroyed for a lack of discipline. Just as an earthly father gives instruction to keep his children safe, so your heavenly father wants you to experience the joys of being his child, but that also comes with receiving his correction!

Pray

Dear God, I humble myself under your leadership. This can be hard for me at times. Help me to be quick to submit. Give me the ability to see the outcome of any act of disobedience before I go down that path. Where I have fallen, please forgive me! I ask for eyes to see your discipline as an act of love and not dis-ownership. Now that I know that you correct those you love; I am grateful for a father that wants what is best for me. Help me to be a self-disciplined person that walks in self-control as a result of your loving discipline.

In Jesus name, Amen

Reflect

❖ How can living a self-disciplined life keep me from the results of poor decisions?

❖ How does knowing God corrects those he loves help me to embrace your discipline?

Meditate

For the Spirit God gave us does not make us timid, but gives us power, love and selfdiscipline. −2 Timothy 1:7

Whoever heeds discipline shows the way to life, but whoever ignores correction leads others astray. −Proverbs 10:17

Folly is bound up in the heart of a child, but the rod of discipline will drive it far away. −Proverbs 22:15

Day 9

God's Discernment

For the word of God is alive and active. Sharper than any double-edged sword, it penetrates even to dividing soul and spirit, joints and marrow; it judges the thoughts and attitudes of the heart.
–Hebrews 4:12 (NIV)

Life can be rather tricky to maneuver. There are the goals we pursue and the sin that pursues us. There's the race we want to run and the oil spills and pot holes that trip us up. It can seem like a constant balancing act. With all these distractions who can really discern right from wrong? God can! And you can too as His child. The bible says "There is a way that seem right to man but the end is death." One of the main differences between God and man is that God looks at the heart, able to see the motives behind an action. Discernment helps us to know what is wise and wisdom helps you to do it. We need the discernment of God in order to avoid the pitfalls of life. We have to trust Him as our counselor and coach. Heb. 4:15 says "For we do not have a high priest who is unable to empathize with our weakness, but we have one who has been tempted in every way, just as we are-yet He did not sin." The truth is Jesus has been where we are and has successfully navigated it all. He understands our weaknesses and our temptations and wants to give us a game plan to win. If we walk thoughtlessly through life, we will never understand the will of God and how to walk in it. We must be wise and discerning, making the most of our time here on earth. Eph. 5:15-17 So, let's ask God for his discernment to walk in the wisdom He provides.

Pray

Father God, help me to walk in discernment. I need to understand the difference between what feels right and what is actually right. I know that you look past my actions to the motives of my heart. Please give me a heart set in your word and help my actions to line up with your will for my life. I'm grateful that you know how difficult it is to know "what" to do and then actually do it. It gives me peace that I am not alone and that you care. Since you were able to live this life and not sin, it gives me hope that I can do the same.

In Jesus name, Amen

Reflect

❖ What noise do I need to clear out to discern God's voice?

❖ How can knowing God's heart help me to experience His peace?

Meditate

Who is wise? Let them realize these things. Who is discerning? Let them understand. The ways of the LORD are right; the righteous walk in them, but the rebellious stumble in them. –Hosea 14:9

And this is my prayer: that your love may abound more and more in knowledge and depth of insight, so that you may be able to discern what is best and may be pure and blameless for the day of Christ, –Phillipians 1:9-10

You discern my going out and my lying down; you are familiar with all my ways. –Psalms 139:3

Day 10

God's Faithfulness

Give thanks to the Lord, for he is good; his love endures forever.

–Psalms 118:1 (NIV)

Faithful is as faithful does, I believe Forest Gump would say, if asked to determine a person's faithfulness. It is in fact a unique quality where seeing is believing. You can't only say you are faithful; you must also show yourself faithful. God is our ultimate example. He has set the sun in the sky and every day without fail it rises and sets. God is a forever God. Because of His steadfast and unchanging nature, we can rely on Him to be there for us and do what He said he would. It's been said that your word is your bond, but in today's world It's hard to find someone that is true to their word. It's because faithfulness requires something from us; honesty, integrity, and perseverance. God will enable us to be truthful to one another and give us an endurance that doesn't quit even when times get tough. Fidelity is the state of being faithful. Some people doubt the fidelity of God due to the infidelity of man. We have to remember that we are Christ's ambassadors on earth; His examples of love and faithfulness. We must seek God for wisdom and strength to live above temptation. When we do, we will set a new precedence of what's acceptable for the next generation. What we put our handprints on today leaves and impression on our tomorrow and impartation on our future. Let us use God's example of faithfulness to inspire us to our own.

Pray

Lord, you are my rock. You remain constant even when everything else begins to change. Your heart toward me is unwavering and your faithfulness in inspiring. Thank you for the example of speaking things into existence and watching over them until they do. Help me to be faithful to you and to your word. Make me stable in all my ways. I desire to be the kind of person that others can rely on. Let faithfulness be the example I set and the legacy I leave.

In Jesus name, Amen

Reflect

- ❖ In what ways have God been faithful to you? Name at least 5.

- ❖ How can being faithful to God and his word bring stability to my life?

Meditate

To declare Your lovingkindness in the morning, And Your faithfulness every night,–Psalms 92:2

God is not human, that he should lie, not a human being, that he should change his mind. Does he speak and then not act? Does he promise and not fulfill? –Numbers 23:19

Because of the LORD's great love we are not consumed, for his compassions never fail. They are new every morning; great is your faithfulness. –Lamentations 3:22-23

My Predestination

Day 11

Who You Are

God made Him who had no sin to be sin for us, so that in Him we might become the righteousness of God.
-2 Corinthians 5:21 (NIV)

Identity is a big deal nowadays, who you are, your likes, dislikes, playlists, and friends, all gives you some type of identity. The world gives you labels by what you do well or what you do wrong. Therefore, we give ourselves an identity by what we identify with. She is dancer, he is a football player. She sleeps around. He is a liar. However, the only way to get from under the blanket of manmade identification is to find out what your creator said you were when He created you. Psalms 139:14 For I am fearfully and wonderfully made. That's a truth you can use to combat any lie from the enemy regarding your identity. You were made intentionally with a specific and great purpose in mind. Eph. 2:10 For we are His workmanship, created in Christ Jesus unto good works, which He prepared in advance for us to do. Refuse to be defined by your past, your portion in life, or even your passion. Instead choose to be redefined by the one who knows you at your core. He says you are righteous. He says you are worthy. He says you are enough. Trust the one that knows you best. He sacrificed His life for you to all He designed you to be. Because of what Jesus did on the cross, old things have passed away and you are a new creation. Trial and temptations come to all; none are exempt. However, the more you identify with your heavenly father by feasting on His word the more you will develop and mature, releasing your truest self.

Pray

Lord, you said I am fearfully and wonderfully made. Help me to see myself the way you do.

Where I have let life and others tell me different, help me to combat those lies with your truth.

You designed me with good things in mind. May I walk in the truth of that understanding. Because of your divine exchange I can begin again as a new creation in you.

In Jesus name, Amen

Reflect

❖ How does knowing who I am in Christ give me power to make necessary changes?

❖ How does knowing the price God paid for me change the way I see my value?

Meditate

Therefore, if anyone is in Christ, the new creation has come: The old has gone, the new is here! –2 Corinthians 5:17

Put on your new nature, created to be like God—truly righteous and holy. –Ephesians 4:24

Day 12

Who You Are Not

And that is what some of you were. But you were washed,
you were sanctified, you were justified in the name of the
Lord Jesus Christ and by the Spirit of our God
1Corinthians 6:11 (NIV)

It is like moving from death to life, like leaving darkness and walking into the light. This new life in Jesus continues to unfold and blossom into something more beautiful with each passing day. It seems impossible that someone could take everything you have ever done wrong and wipe it away as if it never happened. Jesus gives us the example in Luke 7 of two men who owed a debt. One owed five hundred, the other fifty. Since they had no way to pay, the financier cancelled both debts. Then Jesus asked the question, which man do you think was more appreciative? The answer is as simple now as it was back then. The one who was forgiven more. The next time the enemy attempts to rehearse your sins and make you feel unworthy remember God gladly forgave all your sins. He chose you to be his very own, cleansed you and set you apart for His use. "It is the goodness of God that leads men to repentance." Rom. 2:4 It's humbling to think that Jesus paid such a high price to purchase our freedom from sin. It should lead us to gratefulness and repentance. We live in this world but we don't have to live as if we're of this world. You were created with and for a higher purpose. It's that reason that your enemy places detours and roadblocks in your way. He doesn't want you to fulfill your purpose, but Jesus has already taken into account your past, present, and future and He still chose you! So, you are free to let go of who you are not and walk in who you really are.

Day 13

Who's In Control

Then God blessed them and said, "Be fruitful, and multi-
ply. Fill the earth, and govern it. Reign over the fish in the
sea, the birds in the sky, and all the animals that scurry
along the ground."
—Genesis 1:28 (NLT)

I do not know a person that does not want to be in control. Control is the power to exercise restraining ability on or directing influence over, basically to rule. In the beginning we were commanded and given the awesome job of ruling over everything God had created. Everything was subject to our authority. After some craftiness of the enemy we gave up that power. It doesn't take long to look at our world today and see this is not what God envisioned. He made us to reign! Unfortunately, in order to reign we must also hold the reigns. It's the blessing and the burden of being God called and accountable. God says to whom much is given, much is also required. The hardest control to master is self-control. Jesus teaches us how to use our authority wisely. He has given us authority to tread on serpents and scorpions and overcome all the power of the enemy; nothing will harm us. Luke 10:19 The true test of authority is not to use it for evil but for good. Use your authority to fight the enemy of your soul and win. Use your authority to choose life instead of the things that bring destruction. We must understand that there is only one supreme God and that our authority is a delegated one. He is the source and the supply! Since every knee will bow. Philippians 2:10 Let those of us with authority recognize and respect His authority. Submit to His control and watch how you begin to reign in life!!

Pray

Lord, I humble myself to your authority. I understand that all authority is given by you and that it's my job to use it wisely. It's not always easy to bear this kind of weight and sometimes I want to forget my responsibility and just do what I want. Give me the spirit of self-control and help me to mature so that I don't give my power away or use it to lord over others. You have called me to reign in life. I have power to conquer the enemies of my soul and authority to walk in victory in every area of my life. As I intentionally submit to your authority may I consistently begin to walk in my own.

In Jesus name, Amen

Reflect

❖ In what ways do I need to relinquish control?

❖ How can submitting to God's authority free me to walk in my own?

Meditate

Humble yourselves before the Lord, and he will lift you up. –James 4:10

If anyone speaks, they should do so as one who speaks the very words of God. If anyone serves, they should do so with the strength God provides, so that in all things God may be praised through Jesus Christ. To him be the glory and the power for ever and ever. Amen. –1 Peter 4:11

And lead us not into temptation, but deliver us from the evil one.' –Matthew 6:13

Day 14

Who Loves You?

For I am convinced that neither death nor life neither angels nor demons, neither present nor the future, nor any powers, neither height nor depth, nor anything else in all creation, will be able to separate us from the love of God that is in Christ Jesus our Lord.
                    –Romans 8:38-39 (NIV)

Life can feel like a game of tic-tac-toe. Trying to line up your x's and o's so that you can win. And what's the prize? Love, worth, praise. Depending on others to give you love or trying to win love is a fruitless endeavor. People can be fickle, one day they love you and the next they don't. Relying on that kind of love will breath instability into your life. It's the reason there are so many commas in this passage. We as people question God's love for us. We wonder if there are conditions on which God will cease to love us. However, God clearly shows and proves his own love for us by the fact that while we were yet sinners Christ died for us. Rom. 5:8 His love is a true love, not one dependent or conditioned based on our actions. You will never find another that loves you the way God does. We were made to receive love and also give love out but there are misconceptions of what it means to show love. 1 Corinthians 13 teaches us how love should behave. It is patience and kind, not jealous or proud, not selfseeking, not easily angered, does not rejoice in doing wrong but rejoices in doing right. Now before you put someone else picture beside this description, look at yourself. Are you selfseeking and out for what is only good and right for you? Have you rejoiced at sinning and getting away with it? If so, that is not love. Love is self-sacrificing John 3:16 For God so loved the world that He gave His one and only Son that whosoever believes in Him should not perish but have everlasting life. We can receive God's sacrificial love but it's another thing to exhibit our appreciation by giving our lives back to him the way He gave his life to and for us. Don't become like a swimmer that chooses to only sit in the boat, in order to swim you must be in the water. Jump into God's love.

48

Day 15

What Do You Want?

Take delight in the Lord, and he will give you the desires of your heart.

-Psalms 37:4 (NIV)

Personal happiness is one of the strongest desires people have. We are willing to lie, cheat, even steal in order to make ourselves happy. The world teaches us to play along to get along. We try to create our own happiness instead of doing it God's way. King David once saw a married woman bathing and crafted a plan to have her. Once she became pregnant, he tried to cover up his sin, even going to the point of causing her husband's death. You may be wondering; how could a noble man fall so fast? However, we all could face the same fate if we don't temper our desires with a healthy dose of the fear of the Lord. It is the fear of the Lord and a respectful awe that leads to wise decision making. We all have wants and desires but if those desires lead us to disrespect our Lord, they are not worth it! 1 Cor. 10:23a "I have the right to do anything, you say -but not everything is beneficial" Ask God to give you a hunger for the things of God, that you might be too full from the His goodness to eat from the foolishness of the world. Any mom will tell you that if you fill up on foolishness then you will not want real food. If we really want to be happy, we should stay away from evil and pursue the good life that brings us peace.

Pray

Lord, you said you would give me the desires of my heart. Help my desires to line up with your will. Where my own happiness has led me to make questionable decisions, please bring healing. I choose to put your truth over my temperament. Lord I desire long life and good days. I thank you that your word has given me a recipe for success. As I seek and pursue you, may it manifest a peace and a desire for the things of God.

In Jesus name, Amen

Reflect

❖ In what ways have I let my desire dictate my life?

❖ How can nurturing an appetite for the things of God bring me peace?

Meditate

As the deer pants for streams of water, so my soul pants for you, my God. My soul thirsts for God, for the living God. When can I go and meet with God? –Psalm 42:1-2

Whom have I in heaven but you? And earth has nothing I desire besides you. –Psalm 73:25

I take joy in doing your will, my God, for your instructions are written on my heart." –Psalm 40:8

Day 16

What Has Your Heart?

For where your treasure is, there your heart will be also.
—Luke 12:34 (NIV)

It's a funny thing how we determine worth. Something big and elaborate can mean nothing to us and something small, seemingly worthless could mean everything. The reason for this is because worth is based on the value, we give it. You've heard the phrase: one man's trash is another man's treasure". Well it is a good example of how worth and value work together. There are junk yards, resale shops, and garages full of things people no longer find valuable. Jesus understands this concept, in fact he engineered and mastered it. He saw you whom the world; family, friends, coworker, and neighbors' thought were insignificant, but he saw your true value. See to him, you are a one of a kind, sell all you have to get kind of a prize. He knew what others did not and because you had his heart, he gave up all his heavenly wealth to make you His greatest treasure. What things or people have your heart? What have you sacrificed everything to obtain only to find that it was not sustaining? God wants us to enjoy good things Luke 12:23 And although he wants you to eat, drink, and be merry, he desires you to know that those things are not the optimal prize in this life. When we look at the news, we can tell that this world is crumbling. We have to take stock and see where we have invested our life; whether in the pleasures of this world or God's kingdom where there is a treasure built up. Matt 12:35… If you realize that you have sown into things with no lasting value do a reallocation and began to invest in the things that bring an eternal reward. Put your whole heart in it because where your treasure is, there your heart will be also!

Day 17

At What Price?

You were bought at a price; do not become slaves of human beings.

-1 Corinthians 7:23

Redemption is the action of regaining possession of something in exchange for payment. It is the very thing Christ did when he paid his life as payment for our sins. Although it was the highest price anyone could ever pay you were worth it to him. The price that Jesus paid for us was such a daunting task that the Bible says Rom. 5:7-8 Very rarely will anyone die for a righteous person, though for a good person someone might possibly dare to die. But God demonstrates his own love for us in this: While we were still sinners, Christ died for us. The word slavery can have a very negative connotation and with the world's history, who would blame you for thinking the same. However, when the Bible talks about being a slave to God it is talking about giving God lordship authority over your life. We have allowed people and things to lead us around, why not someone worthy of being followed. Living to please only yourself can carry a heavy cost and consequences. They say hindsight is 20/20. If you look at the decision you have made and actions that came before and after many would go back and change something. Why is that? Because they realize that the pleasure was not worth the pain it cost. The truth is we were slaves to our own lust, doing whatever they wanted us to do. However, God invites us to be his servants and serve His purpose that leads to good rewards. Either way, it will cost you your life. Sin is a hard task master. Luring you then trapping you into its never-ending cycle. But Jesus is a servant leader, he demonstrates and then he leads you into servanthood. Then you are only bound to the bond you have to the one that saved you, delivered you, and set you free. Count up all your chips and then put them in, bet on Jesus, He is worth the price!

Pray

Lord Jesus, thank you for setting the example of going all in with God. Your leadership shows me how to serve the only one worthy of my servitude. People and my own desires have lulled me into submission but I declare I will not be mastered by them. You have redeemed me and saved me from the ultimate consequences of my own sin. When I am a slave to sin, I lose myself but when I submit myself to you, I find who I really am. Let it be my heart's desire to sacrifice all I am for you like you sacrificed all you were for me.

In Jesus name, Amen

Reflect

❖ How does knowing God was willing to give His life for you inspire you to live a life of servitude?

❖ In what ways can I submit my life sacrificially?

Meditate

It is for freedom that Christ has set us free. Stand firm, then, and do not let yourselves be burdened again by a yoke of slavery. –Galatians 5:1

So, if the Son sets you free, you will be free indeed. –John 8:36

Well then, should we keep on sinning so that God can show us more and more of his wonderful grace? Of course not! Since we have died to sin, how can we continue to live in it? –Romans 6:1-2

Day 18

When Can I See You Again?

Discretion will guard you, Understanding will watch over you, to deliver you from the way of evil, From the man who speaks perverse things.
–Proverbs 2:11-12 (NASB)

What do you do when you get the call, the request, the invitation to partake in sin again? Will you give in or stand strong? It can be a hard decision to make, especially if you have to do it alone. But thank God he doesn't leave us defenseless. We must arm ourselves with the word of God in order to combat the enemy's temptation. Eph 6 instructs us to put on the full armor of God that we may be able to stand against the wiles of the enemy. Words have a sneaky way of infiltrating our minds and hearts and it is one reason the enemy uses flattery and soothing words to lure us astray. It is better to have a firm stance than and undecided one when sin comes knocking. 1Peter 5:8 Be alert and of sober mind. Your enemy the devil prowls around like a roaring lion looking for someone to devour." Our part is to resist him, standing firm in our faith because you know that the family of believers throughout the whole world are undergoing the same kind of sufferings. This has helped me so many times in life, knowing that I'm not alone and that other brothers and sisters in Christ have had to deal with the same things as I do. This is why it is so important to be rooted in God's word and also in godly relationships. In life there will be people that want the best for you and those that only want the best from you! You have to weed out the takers, the ones when you leave them you come back with less and less. Less consciousness to sin, less respect for God's word, less confidence that God can still use you. Instead, get with people that will build you up and encourage a true walk with God. The key to staying on the right path is living according to God's word. The blessing of living for God is that He will give you the wisdom to escape the next time sin calls your name.

Pray

Lord Jesus, I have answered sins call too many times. It seems to always promise more but leaves me with less. I don't want to be a slave to its smooth words anymore! Thank you for showing me that I have options. Please fill me with your truth so that I have the strength to say No. I will put on the full armor everyday as my battle gear and I choose to walk with the godly since I know there is strength in numbers. Most of all I will be alert to his tactics and depend on you to stand strong.

In Jesus name, Amen

Reflect

❖ How can knowing the truth about sin empower me to say No to it?

❖ Does the company I keep encourage or discourage me to stand strong?

❖ What options do I have, when sin sends an invitation?

Meditate

No temptation has overtaken you except what is common to mankind. And God is faithful; he will not let you be tempted beyond what you can bear. But when you are tempted, he will also provide a way out so that you can endure it. –1 Corinthians 10:13

Submit yourselves, then, to God. Resist the devil, and he will flee from you. –James 4:7

So, I say, walk by the Spirit, and you will not gratify the desires of the flesh. –Galatians 5:16

Day 19

When's Your Time?

There is a time for everything, and a season for every activity under the heavens:
-Ecclesiastes. 3:1 (NIV)

Timing is everything! It determines when you wake up and when you go to bed. There are only twenty-four hours in a day, and when it's gone, its gone. It's up to us to use our time wisely.

Psalm 90:12 "Teach us to number our days, that we may gain a heart of wisdom." We so need wisdom in order for us to not waste our time. When we come to the end of our lives, we don't want to regret the precious time we let slip through our fingers. If God has a plan for our life and we have an allotted time to accomplish it, then we have to get moving. Many things can sidetrack you and cause you to waste time. Sin will send you on a rabbit trail always jumping after the next desire, however God know what you really need and will provide all of your needs in his time. Instead of trying to make things happen on your own seek God first and then the other things will come. Waiting can be trying but there is normally a lesson that can be learned while waiting and God is faithful. He will not put more of you that you can bear. While you are waiting, if it seems unbearable, remember His grace is sufficient to help you until your change comes. There is a blessing in living and loving God's way. Prob 10:22 "The blessing of the LORD brings wealth, without painful toil for it." We can choose to waste our time on worldly happiness and have nothing but sorrow to show for it or we can use our time for God' agenda and receive the rewards of joy and peace that last beyond our time on this earth. It's time to make a decision. It's your time!

Pray

Father God, I realize that time is a gift from you. Help me to use my time wisely. Forgive me where I have wasted it on things that brought me no value. I ask you to please redeem the time so that I can live more purposefully moving forward. Thank you for being so patient with me especially when I ran out and did things my own way. Help me to trust your timing in all things and get in alignment with your timing. I know that if I seek you first, everything else will be added to me in due time.

In Jesus name, Amen

Reflect

- ❖ How does knowing this life is a gift bring focus and intentionality to the decisions I make?

- ❖ What ways can I use my time wisely to positively affect the lives of others?

Meditate

I have brought you glory on earth by finishing the work you gave me to do. –John 17:4

Be very careful, then, how you live--not as unwise but as wise, –Ephesians 5:15

And do this, understanding the present time: The hour has already come for you to wake up from your slumber, because our salvation is nearer now than when we first believed. –Romans 13:11

Day 20

When the Trumpet Sounds

For the Lord himself will come down from heaven, with a loud command, with the voice of the archangel and with the trumpet call of God, and the dead in Christ will rise first.
- 1 Thessalonians 4:16 (NIV)

We were made to reign and be a part of God's holy family. What a glorious appointment! It only makes sense that when the King of kings returns, it will be with a trumpets call. Trumpets are used in the military to send clear communication in the midst of confusion. They also signify events and times of worship. When Jesus returns a second time it will be to cumulate what he has already set in motion. Everything we need to defeat sin has already been done. He has given us every weapon we need to fight the enemy and win. God is expecting for us to grow in our faith. Heb. 5:14 But solid food is for the mature, who by constant use have trained their senses to distinguish good from evil." We can stay in our sin and our excuses for them; and yes, God would still love us but oh how so much time we would have wasted. Instead let us give ownership of our lives over to God and be ready for His next move. He is an extraordinary God with great plans for you all the way into eternity. Let's be ready for the trumpets call.

Pray

Father God, you are coming back for your children. Thank you for the inheritance of being a part of your kingdom Help me to shed the weight of anything that holds me down so that I can be free to run with you. You are developing me to be ready for your return. I declare a maturity within me to put away childish things and embrace what full grown men and women enjoy. Lord you said that those that lived for you in this life would reap eternal rewards. Let that be my hearts resolve as I wait in anticipation of your return.

In Jesus Name, Amen

Reflect

❖ What things can I let go of so I'm available to receive the gift you have for me?

❖ What areas is God developing in me to be ready to embrace my new life in Christ?

Meditate

And if I go and prepare a place for you, I will come back and take you to be with me that you also may be where I am. –John 14:3

Let us be glad and rejoice, and let us give honor to him. For the time has come for the wedding feast of the Lamb, and his bride has prepared herself. –Revelation 19:7-9

So, you also must be ready, because the Son of Man will come at an hour when you do not expect him. –Matthew 24:44

Others' Perfection

Day 21

We Need Each Other

As iron sharpens iron, so one person sharpens another
-Proverbs 27:17 (NIV)

There is nothing more comforting than a good friend, someone that can hear you out and give you honest feedback. We were made for relationship. When God made man, He said it was not good for him to be alone. Pride may lead us to believe that we can do it on our own but we can accomplish so much more together. Eccl. 4:9 Two are better than one, because they have a good return for their labor. At times our perspective of each other can be distorted and instead of seeing one another as a brother or sister in Christ, we see them as a means to satisfy our own selfish desires. In essence, we are using them. We must get past our need for immediate gratification and look forward to the God given purpose for each person. Since we have a real enemy, we have to refuse to be used as an instrument to bring each other down. We were meant to bring restoration, healing, and support. (Gal. 6:1) There is healing in community. When we confess our sins to one another and carry each other burdens it brings a welcome relief. Although wear and tear from the world can make us dull, pure fellowship can keep us sharp and give us the edge we need to accomplish our God given goals.

Pray

Father God, from the beginning you have made us to do life together. Partnering with each other to accomplish your God-given agenda. Strengthen the relationships in my life to resemble what you have intended. Lord, where I have taken a bond out of context or used others to satisfy my own selfish needs, please forgive me. Give me a clear perspective so I am not blinded by my own desires. I pray for unity in order to bring restoration and healing. Use us to sharpen one another in a positive way to bring about the best version of ourselves and others.

In Jesus name, Amen

Reflect

❖ How does knowing that we are partners in God's plan change how I view others?

❖ In what ways can I move from my selfish perspective of "me" to a constructive "we"?

Meditate

The LORD God said, "It is not good for the man to be alone. I will make a helper suitable for him." –Genesis 2:18

Bear with each other and forgive one another if any of you has a grievance against someone. Forgive as the Lord forgave you –Colossians 3:13

Confess your sins to each other and pray for each other so that you may be healed. The earnest prayer of a righteous person has great power and produces wonderful results. –James 5:16

Day 22

We Belong To Each Other

Now you are the body of Christ, and each one of you is a part of it.
– I Corinthians 12:27 (NIV)

Have you ever seen a root-less, branch-less, leaf-less, or bark-less tree? No, of course not! It may be a stick or possibly a stump, but by no means is it a tree. The same way a tree is not a tree without its parts, so are you not complete without your family in Christ. When people see you, they can tell where you came from. We are all created in God's image, but we lose our productivity by not being connected to the rest of God's body. Heb 10:24 "Let us think of ways to motivate one another to acts of love and good works." Our job is to encourage one another so that together we may be a force to be reckoned with. As the body, we are the hands and feet of Christ bringing restoration and healing to a hurting world. We all have specific gifts and callings to be used for God's glory. We must find out what ours is and then get busy doing it! We cannot afford to be idle. Think about how you have watched your favorite team win a game due to everyone playing their role to the best of their ability. That's how God wants His family to act, like a winning team! Though it might be simpler to do life alone, its so much more rewarding to do it together. No one wants to carry all the load. Jesus said "The harvest is plentiful, but the laborers are few." Matt. 9:37. You are the missing piece in a much larger puzzle. So, align your life with the will of God because your contribution is vital to the success of all.

Pray

Lord, thank you for the revelation that I am not an island. There are no individual actions that don't have corresponding reactions. Forgive me for trying to live alone, pretending that what I do only affects me. Help me reconnect to the unit and begin walking in step with it. Because you have given me a unique calling, I don't want to become idle but an active contributor to the work at hand. As we bring all our parts together, may we accomplish infinitely more that we could have ever done alone. Help us to ascribe value to one another and not play the comparison game that undermine our common goal.

In Jesus name, Amen

Reflect

❖ In what ways have I separated myself physically or spiritually from the body of Christ?

❖ How can I build an ebb and flow relationship with other that benefits the body as a whole?

Meditate

The body is a unit, though it is composed of many parts. And although its parts are many, they all form one body. So it is with Christ –1 Corinthians 12:12

And let us consider how to spur one another on to love and good deeds. Let us not neglect meeting together, as some have made a habit, but let us encourage one another, and all the more as you see the Day approaching. –Hebrews 10:24-25

Two are better than one, because they have a good return for their labor: –Ecclesiastes 4:9-10

Day 23

We Affect Each Other

If one part suffers, every part suffers with it; if one part is
honored, every part rejoices with it.
-1 Corinthians 12:26 (NIV)

A rock thrown in a pond has a ripple effect. The one impact has been felt by the surrounding waters. Just like that pebble, no matter how small you feel your contribution or lack thereof, you are a part of something larger than yourself. Many people believe they can do whatever they want to do and that it only affects themselves. But you only have to ask someone stuck in sin how their work and family relationships have suffered because of it. A headache can make a whole body shut down, just the same, a cheerful heart can give energy to the entire body. The truth is, you get to decide what affect you have on the body. Lack of honesty and transparency can cause us to do life alone. But true healing comes when we open up about our issues. James 5:16 "Therefore confess your sins to each other and pray for each other so that you may be healed. The prayer of a righteous person is powerful and effective." God wants us to be whole and though He is in control, He likes to work through men. God says we are his ambassadors on earth and we want to represent him well by impacting one another in positive ways.

Pray

Lord, whether I like it or not we are all interconnected. Once I accepted you as my savior I was engrafted into your family. The beauty is that I no longer have to do life alone, but now I have to willfully mature since I have someone depending on me. Holy Spirit, help me to be transparent in confessing where I have messed up so I can be healed. May we be compassionate to one another knowing that our life is not our own and we are in this together.

In Jesus name, Amen

Reflect

❖ How can I live more self-aware of the impact my life has on others?

❖ Do I have someone that I can openly share my issues without fear?

Meditate

Therefore, confess your sins to each other and pray for each other so that you may be healed. The prayer of a righteous person is powerful and effective. –James 5:16

Let each of you look out not only for his own interests, but also for the interests of others. –Philippians 2:4

Let us not become weary in doing good, for at the proper time we will reap a harvest if we do not give up. –Galatians 6:9-10

Day 24

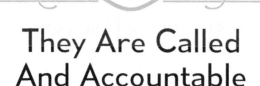

They Are Called
And Accountable

So then, each of us will give an account of ourselves to God.

–Romans 14:12 (NIV)

Accidents occur when one or both parties are not paying attention. When the authorities arrive, someone is normally determined to be at-fault. Many times, the consequences include taking defensive driving; a course designed to make the party responsible more careful and aware of others on the road. Our duty as believers is to go beyond our individual lives to reach those around us. When we cast blame; we minimize our faults and maximize others flaws. Matt 7:4 How can you say to your brother, 'Let me take the speck out of your eye,' when all the time there is a plank in your own eye?" The first step in accountability is self-awareness.

We cannot control others, we can only control what we choose to do. There is already enough standing in the way of believers trying to live for God, we have to refuse to be used as a tool in tripping each other up. Let us live our lives defensively and thereby causing less accidents along the way. When we refocus our eyes on God, we allow others to accomplish so much more.

Pray

Lord, we must all stand before you and give an account for the life we lived. I cannot blame others for the choices I made nor can I be used as an excuse for others. Since you are the only real judge, help me to stop criticizing and critiquing and to start praying and doing my part to help my brothers and sisters. Set my life on the right course so that I may be a light on the path instead of a roadblock in their way. Help me to be more aware of my own short comings so that I can ask you to work on me to make my own calling sure. Help me to live in such a way that my actions not only help me but also protects those around me.

In Jesus name, Amen

Reflect

❖ What choices can I make to be more accountable to God and others?

❖ Who can I pray for instead of criticizing today?

Meditate

Brothers and sisters, if someone is caught in a sin, you who live by the Spirit should restore that person gently. But watch yourselves, or you also may be tempted. Carry each other's burdens, and in this way, you will fulfill the law of Christ. –Galatians 6:1-2

Be kind and compassionate to one another, forgiving each other, just as in Christ God forgave you.–Ephesians 4:32

You, then, why do you judge your brother or sister? Or why do you treat them with contempt? For we will all stand before God's judgment seat –Romans 14:10

Therefore, my brothers and sisters, make every effort to confirm your calling and election. For if you do these things, you will never stumble, –2 Peter 1:10

Day 25

They Are Custom Made

For you formed my inward parts, you knitted me together in my mother's womb. I praise you, for I am fearfully and wonderfully made.

–Psalms 139:13-14 (ESV)

The Last Supper by Leonardo DaVinci, The Creation of Adam by Michael Angelo were both handcrafted paintings by their creators. The world marvels at the handiwork of men that will eventually parish. How much more will they marvel when we accomplish the good works God prepared for us to do? Though we look similar, we are not the same. We were all created with a specific purpose in mind. Holy - is seen as a scary word to some. It is either considered super spiritual or unattainable. To be holy only means to be set apart for God's service. Rom12:1 "And so, dear brothers and sisters, I plead with you to give your bodies to God because of all he has done for you. Let them be a living and holy sacrifice—the kind he will find acceptable. This is truly the way to worship him." It is God that gave us these bodies, our breath, and provides for our daily needs. Shouldn't we use our bodies to glorify him? Why do we constantly use or bodies for things that bring dishonor to ourselves and the demise of others? Just like you, they were created in God's image for good works. Once we understand our value to God, we'll stop undervaluing ourselves and others. We were tailor made to fulfill a purpose that only we can accomplish. Let us cut the strings that trip us up and walk boldly in the path that leads us to our destiny.

Pray

Father God, thank you for taking the time to craft us all as unique human beings. We were intentionally created with your purpose in mind. Help us to see the true value in one another and not just what we can get from each other. As recipients of your grace, may we set ourselves apart from selfish desires and begin walking in the plan you have for us. It has been said that if you don't know the purpose of a thing, misuse in inevitable. Give us a proper perspective of your creation that we may be an encouragement to others to reach their fullest potential.

In Jesus name, Amen

Reflect

❖ How can I honor God and others with my body?

❖ What would it look like to set myself apart for God's use and embrace my holiness?

Meditate

So, God created mankind in his own image, in the image of God he created them; male and female he created them. –Genesis 1:27

For we are God's handiwork, created in Christ Jesus to do good works, which God prepared in advance for us to do. –Ephesians 2:10

Yet you, LORD, are our Father. We are the clay, you are the potter; we are all the work of your hand. –Isaiah 64:8

Day 26

They Are Counting On You

We who are strong ought to bear with the failings of the
weak and not to please ourselves.
                                        –Rom 15:1 (NIV)

Parents are God's way of seeing that children get cared for. As babies they need us constantly, but as they grow their needs advance. You are no longer needed for basic care but for more complex situations. If parents are the bedrock of the family, then brother and sisters are the community in which we do life. Prov.17:17 A friend loves at all times, and a brother is born for a time of adversity. When hard times come, we look to people we can depend on. You are someone's brother or sister in Christ and they are looking to you for support. It's disappointing when instead of healthy support they find someone that will take advantage of their misfortune. Pure motives are needed and guards put in place to ensure they are properly cared for. Gal. 6:1 "Brothers and sisters, if someone is caught in a sin, you who live by the Spirit should restore that person gently. But watch yourselves, or you also may be tempted." They are counting on you to stand strong and to help them out of the mess they are in. Ask God to give you a pure perspective toward your family in Christ. It may be easier said than done, but it is possible and important to remember that they are depending on you for safe relationships. Let's seek God's best for one another and be willing to put them first and not just do what is convenient for us.

Pray

Lord, it's not easy to maintain pure motives in today's world. There is so much drawing us away internally as well as externally. We need your power to stand strong. Thank you for showing us that we can't just believe to do right, we need an actual plan. Help us to place guardrails in our relationships so we know when we are running the risk of crashing. Give us the right mindset toward our brothers and sisters. Let us make our father proud by supporting them and not stunting their progress.

In Jesus name, Amen

Reflect

❖ What guardrails can I put in place so that I support my brother and sister when they need me?

❖ Do I have any healthy relationship that I can model after?

Meditate

Treat older women as you would your mother, and treat younger women with all purity as you would your own sisters. –Timothy 5:2

Do to others as you would have them do to you. –Luke 6:31

Do your best to present yourself to God as one approved, a worker who does not need to be ashamed and who correctly handles the word of truth. –Timothy 2:15

In the same way, urge the younger men to be self-controlled. In everything, show yourself to be an example by doing good works. In your teaching show integrity, dignity, and wholesome speech that is above reproach, so that anyone who opposes us will be ashamed to have nothing bad to say about us. –Titus 2:6-7

Day 27

They're Capable Continuation

Do you not know that in a race all the runners run, but only one gets the prize? Run in such a way as to get the prize.
-1 Corinthians 9:24 (NIV)

Runners train their entire lives to race. They visualize themselves running well, hitting landmarks, and finishing strong. I do not know a runner that does not want to win. But unfortunately, many runners get distracted and fall short of reaching their goals. Gal 5:7 You were running a good race. Who cut in on you to keep you from obeying the truth?

If we are not careful, we can be used as bait to lure people away from the truth. Unsubmitted sin cannot only impede our process but also obstruct others. We must submit our sin on the cross of Christ and be filled with the knowledge of His will in all we do. There is nothing more harmful to a runner that self-doubt. Just like a runner, when our brothers or sisters fall, they can start to doubt their worthiness. We want people to win their race and not short circuit their victory. If anything, we want to encourage them to get back in the race and to keep on running. We must use our power to lift one another up and encourage them to run-on to receive their prize.

Pray

Lord, help us to finish strong. Many times, we start a thing but lack the will to see it through. Give us the tenacity to run our race and not be distracted from our course. We have a responsibility to make sure others have the same capabilities to pursue and accomplish their goals. Let our lives breed encouragement and breathe life into those that want to give up. May our presence promote healing and reignite a determination to pursue the prize.

In Jesus name, Amen

Reflect

❖ How can I minimize the distractions that take others off course?

❖ In what ways can I encourage others to reach their full potential?

Meditate

And I am certain that God, who began the good work within you, will continue his work until it is finally finished on the day when Christ Jesus returns. –Philippians 1:6

Therefore, since we are surrounded by such a huge crowd of witnesses to the life of faith, let us strip off every weight that slows us down, especially the sin that so easily trips us up. And let us run with endurance the race God has set before us. –Hebrews 12:1

I have fought the good fight, I have finished the race, I have kept the faith. –2 Timothy 4:7

Day 28

Our Combined Purpose

For he chose us in him before the creation of the world to
be holy and blameless in his sight in love.
–Ephesians 1:4 (NIV)

Unity is a beautiful thing to witness. A choir is better that one singer, an army; stronger than one soldier, a neighborhood; greater that one home. With unity comes power. Power to build up and power to tear down. 2 Cor. 10:4 The weapons of our warfare are not the weapons of the world. Instead, they have divine power to demolish strongholds. Attaining the goal of being holy and blameless in God's sight is a fight! Our purpose is to build God's kingdom and tear down the enemies. With purpose comes opposition, but we were not meant to fight alone. As the saying goes... there is strength in numbers and we need every member doing their part. When we pray for and with each other that is when God's power goes to work. The effectual, fervent prayer of the righteous avails much. We will see victory when we work together. We will not leave anyone out or leave any behind. Jesus tells the story of the one sheep that went missing, He describes how he left the 99 in search of the one, and how he rejoiced over that one once he was found. Why fret over one when you still have 99? Well, it's because our God loves us all so much that He doesn't want anyone to miss out on the good things He has prepared for them. Let's share His heart by working together to build His kingdom, and enjoy our inheritance together!

Pray

Father God, you have chosen us before the foundation of the world for a unique purpose. Thank you for the dominion we possess when we walk in unity. Help us to see that we are stronger together. We will no longer allow the enemy to pick us apart. Bind us so that we are able to conquer our common enemy and walk in our inheritance as children of God.

In Jesus name, Amen

Reflect

❖ How could I be stronger in my faith by I joining forces with other believers?

❖ What victories would I like to see in the world if the body of Christ worked together effectively?

❖ What part do I play and bringing unity especially to those that feel left out?

Meditate

This will continue until we all come to such unity in our faith and knowledge of God's Son that we will be mature in the Lord, measuring up to the full and complete standard of Christ. –Ephesians 4:13

Then make me truly happy by agreeing wholeheartedly with each other, loving one another, and working together with one mind and purpose. –Philippians 2:2

May the God who gives endurance and encouragement give you the same attitude of mind toward each other that Christ Jesus had, so that with one mind and one voice you may glorify the God and Father of our Lord Jesus Christ. –Romans 15:5-6

Day 29

Our Collective Efforts

Two are better than one, because they have a good return
for their labor
                                        –Ecclesiastes 4:9 (NIV)

Partnership is where parties agree to cooperate to advance a shared interest. Great partnerships can be seen in business, music, and even the literary world. It's when you strike a balance in saying, separate we are good, but together we are great. Partnerships take patience and constant communication to be effective. When they are working well, they are a thing to be admired. This is the type of togetherness; God wants for us. We take our strengths and weakness and make something beautiful. God wants to use the body of Christ to effect change into the world. The job is too big for one person or group, it takes us all to impact the world for Jesus. One thing that can bring division is offense. When we are offended, it hinders our ability to work together. We begin to see one another as enemies instead of partners and friends. The real enemy likes to sow discord amongst believers so that our efforts will be divided with everyone going their own way. Psalm 133:1 says "How wonderful and pleasant it is when brothers live together in harmony! God's desire is that we walk in unity so that collectively we can be and bring about something beautiful. We are not all going to develop at the same pace, so patience will be needed until we all reach maturity in Christ. As we pursue unity let us refuse to be offended and remember that we are better together than we are on our own.

Pray

Father God, we know that one is too small a number to do anything great. Help us to each do our part in building your kingdom. Give us patience with one another. May we communicate well to eliminate misunderstanding and strife. Help us to not let our individuality interfere with our common goal. But let our differences bring a higher level of discernment as we walk in our unified purpose. May our results be multiplied because of our maximized effort in doing it together.

In Jesus name, Amen

Reflect

❖ What areas of pride can I lay down to accomplish God's agenda?

❖ How can combining efforts bring better results than those attempted on my own?

Meditate

I appeal to you, brothers and sisters, in the name of our Lord Jesus Christ, that all of you agree with one another in what you say and that there be no divisions among you, but that you be perfectly united in mind and thought. –1 Cor. 1:10

A person's wisdom yields patience; it is to one's glory to overlook an offense. –Prov. 19:11

Day 30

Our Collaboration is Necessary

For we are co-workers in God's service; you are God's field, God's building.

–1 Corinthians 3:9 (NIV)

The root word for collaboration is co-labor. Meaning to labor together. I'm not sure if you've e ever experienced or witness to a woman in labor. It is a tiring and strenuous activity. Bottom line is, it's a lot of work! People often ask, if it's such a hard task why would anyone do it at all?

The answer is simple, what it brings forth is far more amazing than any pain it took to deliver. We are all in some form of labor. Either nurturing the gift that God has placed inside of us, preparing to give birth, or supporting those in the process. All are needed and all are necessary. In Matt. 18 Jesus' disciples ask who is the greatest in the kingdom of heaven? But Jesus explains that whoever take the position of a child is the greatest in the kingdom of Heaven. It's the enemy's job to breed strife and division through comparison. We think that those that stand out are the ones most favored in God's eyes. But it's those that are humble and stand up for others that get His attention. Working together and doing our part is essential in bringing about God's Kingdom on the earth. In John 17 Jesus prays that we all would be one just as He and the Father are one. It's important in the body of Christ that we quit trying to one up one another and begin collaborating together to bring about a glory that the world has never see.

Pray

Lord, thank you for modeling unity. When you said "Let us make man in our image" we understand that you value relationships. Your desire is that we walk together as one. Help us to understand the mystery of the body of Christ being one body with many parts. May we, as parts of that body find our own unique purpose in it! Remove the temptation to judge and compare. As we move in our individual functions, synchronize our differences that it may be a testimony to the world around us. Let the beauty of this collaboration bring glory to your name and draw others to your kingdom.

In Jesus name, Amen

Reflect

❖ What does it mean for me to be a co-laborer?

❖ What can I contribute in birthing God plan on earth?

❖ How does understanding that we all have a unique and valuable part to play cancel out comparison in the body?

Meditate

Each of you should use whatever gift you have received to serve others, as faithful stewards of God's grace in its various forms. –1 Peter 4:10

How good and pleasant it is when God's people live together in unity! –Psalm 133:1

From him the whole body, joined and held together by every supporting ligament, grows and builds itself up in love, as each part does its work. –Ephesians 4:16

ABOUT THE AUTHOR

Crystal Campbell is graced to be a wife to John and mother of Johanna and John IV. She found her passion for writing when she was young; writing poetry, songs, and journaling. Crystal has always enjoyed putting words together that brought a sense of excitement and understanding. Born in the great state of Texas, she is a University of Houston Alumni. Go Coogs! Losing her mom at a young age and being raised by her father she learned to value the things that really matter in life, to always save for a rainy day, and to make time to laugh often. She is the owner of Crystal Clear Content where she advises and offers services to businesses such as copywriting, editing, blogs, articles, and podcasts. Spending time with her family, listening to music, road trips, kickboxing, and drinking sweet tea are what brings a smile to her face. Crystal loves God and has a passion to see others reach their fullest potential.

Can You Help?

Thank You For Reading My Book!

I really appreciate all of your feedback, and I love hearing what you have to say.

I need your input to make the next version of this book and my future books better.

Please leave me an honest review on Amazon letting me know what you thought of the book.

Thanks so much!

–Crystal Campbell

ρ

Made in the USA
Las Vegas, NV
15 February 2021

17865629R00066